Tax
The
Rich!

The Arguments for Equality, Fairness, and Equal Pay

A Roadmap for Success to the 2016 Presidential Election!

Rich Hand

ISBN-10: 1514782162

ISBN-13: 978-1514782163

DEDICATION

To Anne P. Hand who inspired me to write through her heart felt notes, birthday cards, and letters she authored throughout my life. I will never be as talented with words as she was but it gives me a goal and dream to achieve. Thank you Mom!

CONTENTS

Tax The Rich!

ACKNOWLEDGMENTS

The Founding Fathers are an inspiration, and to anyone interested in protecting minorities and offering opportunities their creation of a republic opened opportunity to everyone by protecting the individual and disregarding birthright privilege. Although they are despised by so many it should be seen as a badge of success. I often feel a connection to the turbulent times they lived and write with the same passion they had for this country. The founder's words have never rung more true than the day they wrote them - and in the world we find ourselves today.

Thank you to my wife who stands by me in all of my pursuits - laughing at me, and with me, making life a pleasure.

I thank my kids, (now adults) for helping me to see from a younger perspective. I appreciate you allowing me to turn everything into a lesson in our founding principles. You will live and learn, and someday, maybe, see why I find understanding human behavior, history and politics so important!

HISTORIC LOOK AT TAX RATES

The top marginal tax rate for the rich in the United States in the 40's and 50's hovered around 90%. So let's look at how that compares to today's top rate of 39%. For the average rich family in America making $100,000 a year, the difference between a 90% tax rate and a 39% rate is significant. The tax burden on the $100,000 wage earner in the 40's and 50's was $90,000. This left the wage earner with $10,000.00 to take care of all of the family needs including food, shelter, and clothing. Today that wage earner would pay $39,000 in taxes. That leaves the wage earner with $61,000 to take care of the family's needs. So the difference is huge between a 90% tax rate and a 39% rate but is it fair?

I am looking forward to presenting the argument for taxing the rich. Why should anyone be allowed to keep what they earn when there are so many people in need? I am going to address the argument of fairness, income inequality, the unfairness of capitalism, privilege, hurdles to educational opportunities, the minimum wage, single parent families, and how taxing the rich is the fairest way to fix the problems we are facing in today's society.

How can we ever expect a fair society unless we take from the rich to give to the poor? Why should someone who has lucked out be able to buy so much more than others that are less fortunate? This is a situation that must be fixed in order to make this country great again.

In order to get started we should take a look at the systemic problem of capitalism. Capitalism is a fundamentally flawed system because it gives an advantage to the rich, people that work harder than others, and those people that work longer hours to make more money. It encourages people to work more instead of living a balanced life where people have time to pursue their passions.

I will make the comparisons between capitalism and socialism, the two competing systems today in America, to prove the point that capitalism encourages people to work hard and socialism gives people more time to do the things they love.

Capitalism Vs Socialism

Everyone knows that Socialism as an economic system treats everyone equally. The US Constitution was designed to create equality for all so why are we not using an economic system like Socialism instead of Capitalism?

Some people are not born rich. The capitalist system favors the rich. You can conclude that because under the system here in the US, capitalism has created more rich people around the world than any other economic system devised by man! If a system is so good at creating a lot of rich people, how can we continue to use such a system with good conscience? In order to create more poor people we need to implement a more socialist system so that everyone is equal and no one can become rich.

The resources that winners in the capitalist system use to become rich are everyone's resources. So why should only some people and not all people benefit? If you look at places that have a socialist system, only a few people get rich. Most people in countries that have a socialist system are equally poor and have little chance to become rich. This is exactly what we want to encourage here to limit the ability of some people to get rich in the first place. We would not have to tax the rich so much if we had less rich people in the first place.

It is often argued that people will not start businesses in a socialist system. Why not? Most people want to work so people will still want to create businesses even if they know they will not get rich. Take for example someone that wants to start a restaurant in a capitalist system compared to in a socialist system.

In a capitalist system, a restaurant owner would take his money and invest it into the things that he/she needs to start a business. The first thing needed is space at a location that will draw enough people to support the restaurant. The entrepreneur has to buy or lease the cooking equipment, computers to run the business, tables chairs, food, liquor, and create and print menus for the patrons. It usually takes tens of thousands of dollars to get the restaurant started.

Once he/she gets everything in place the owner can open the restaurant and start making money to become rich.

In a socialist system, a restaurant owner will use someone else's money to buy the things needed to start the restaurant. He/she will choose a location for the restaurant and since in the socialist system the landlord doesn't need to make a profit. The restaurant owner can find a place to set up at a very low cost. That is the beauty of socialism; no one needs to be rich or care about making money. Other people provide it. The cooking equipment, computers, tables' chairs, food, liquor, and menus are ordered and delivered with the other people's money.

Once he/she gets everything in place the owner opens the restaurant and takes any money made and gives it to the government to share with everyone else. This makes sure no one gets rich and everyone benefits from this person opening the restaurant. The important thing is no one gets rich and everyone shares in the money the restaurant makes.

It is clear that when you compare capitalism to socialism more people become equal in socialism and no one gets rich. Compared to capitalism where so many people get rich and few people get to share the money the restaurant makes, you can see socialism makes people more equal and produces no rich people.

The problem is we live in a capitalist system and in order to make it fair for the most people we have to tax the rich to re-distribute the unfair wealth that gets created through capitalism.

That is why I wrote this book! We have to make the system fairer, and the only way beyond changing the system to socialism is to tax the rich. Taxing the rich will make it fair for everyone.

When people say that capitalism is a fair system I have to ask what is fair about some people getting rich over other people who may not want to work as hard? If someone didn't finish school, would rather be an artist or musician, or live on the street and would rather be homeless, why should they not be treated fairly? Considering that the education system, the roads the restaurant owner (or any other business owner) used to get to school and work were built by the government, they need to share the wealth. That gives a right to all people to share in the wealth of the restaurant owner. No one should have to suffer when there are people that can support them through taxation.

We will look at the many inequalities of America and why we need to tax the rich even more!

Profits

Why do we need profits? Why can't we just rename profits so we can distribute them to the people that need the money? If a company makes more than they need to pay their employees then the rest can be shared for the good of society.

Profits are really just extra money. So if it is extra money, why not just spread it around to all of the people that need it to make things fair?

Profits come from people spending more than they need to for a product or service if you think about it. That means that they were overcharged if there is money left over right? I every business only used the money they received for their products and services to pay the employees and what it costs to make the product or provide the services then all of the extra money could be used to help people that are less fortunate.

Government programs don't make a profit so why should private business? There is so much we could do with extra profits from successful businesses if we only mandated a policy through government to force businesses to hand over more money to the government.

Instead of a few people having a lot of money we could have a lot of people having a little more money. This could actually help private businesses succeed because more people would have money to buy their products and services.

Big Oil

Big oil companies are greedy and destroying the environment. The profits that BO (Big Oil) makes are obscene! These profits must be shared by all in order to make America fairer for all.

How is it fair for oil companies to make so much money from people that need to drive every day to get to school, work, and the gym? How is it moral to charge people so much to heat their homes? If the oil company is making so much in profits, why can't they just lower their prices?

We need to tax oil companies more because of all of the environmental damage they are doing to our planet. The oil companies have to be held responsible for all of the damage they have done over the course of history. In fact if we didn't have oil companies we wouldn't have cars, planes, trains, and factories. We probably would have so much less to worry about if we didn't have big oil companies.

It wouldn't be a bad thing if we taxed oil companies out of existence and replaced it with solar power or candles, or windmills.

If we taxed the rich BO companies and used that money to build more solar panels and windmills, we could end our dependence on oil. I know that someone could create an extension cord long enough to power an electric car to commute to work. If there was a way to invent a retractable cord like the ones we use in vacuum cleaners, we could really sell a lot more electric cars. Sometimes we have to look back to make progress.

Windmills are everywhere you look now a days. This is another example of old technology with a new purpose. These windmills don't make anyone rich because windmills don't make enough energy to replace oil, but the fact that no one can get rich is a good thing. We just have to find a way to make windmills smaller so we can put them on the hood of the car. This way when the car is moving the wind will create the electric power and that power can be used to run the car. It's like a loop of energy! We just have to start at the top of a hill each time until we come up with a way to store wind power. There are definitely smart people that can figure that out since we will have more people going to college because it will be free. That is; If we tax the rich to make college free.

Big Oil is just the tip of the tax iceberg when it comes to taxing rich people and companies. We have to look at Big Insurance. Insurance companies collect a lot of money but then they don't let us use it to buy healthcare with the money they make.

Big Insurance

What is insurance for? Is it to make a profit or to give people the money they need to pay for their car, home, or medical needs? These are questions we must answer if we are going to create policies that help the people.

Let's look at how insurance works. To make it easy we will use Car insurance to understand the way most insurance works. The customer pays a premium to the insurance company when they buy a car so that if something happens to that car the insurance company will pay to fix or replace it. So for example you buy a brand new car and you pay $20,000. If you are one of the 1% and can buy it cash then you can decide the type of insurance you want to pay for. But if you are one of the other 99%, the bank that lends you the money for the car will want to make sure if something happens to that car they protect their investment. I am not sure why the person buying the car should have to pay since the bank makes so much profit, but that subject is for another chapter.

So the person buying the car is forced to pay for an insurance policy every month even though they may have put no money down on the car and have no risk, and the premium can be expensive; $500 - $1200 dollars a year. So the buyer that does not have a lot of money now has to buy insurance from the big bank, after just borrowing $20,000 to pay the big car company, even if nothing ever happens to the car! So if after 5 to 7 years of paying for the car and nothing happens to the car, the insurance company has made huge profits. It might be prudent policy if the government forced the insurance companies to pay back the premium at that point. In socialism, since you don't need to make a profit like capitalism, the company would be able to do that. And that is why we need to change to socialism if we want a more equal society. But I digress.

The CEO of the insurance company makes millions of dollars a year and the guy who bought the car pays his salary. It's like giving money directly to the Republican Party.

If the person that bought the $20,000 car gets in an accident in the first month of owning the car and the car has to be replaced, that is a better deal for the customer. So why not just let people buy insurance when they get in an accident? And shouldn't insurance cover brakes, oil changes, tires, and general repairs if we are going to pay that much for it? We could take it out of the CEO's salary!

You see how big insurance is ripping us off? And the government is being bought by lobbyists to force us to pay for insurance even if we don't want it. That is why we need more politicians to understand how we are getting ripped off by big companies and big Republican donors.

Health Insurance

If you think you are getting ripped off for car insurance, think about health insurance. We all get sick and we all need care and it should be a right! I will talk about that in another chapter because it is in our constitution right under our noses and nobody ever talks about it. But I will!

The health insurance industry is making billions of dollars off the 99% and that is why the government should control healthcare. No company should be allowed to make a profit on our health. If the government controlled healthcare then we could make it free! The government is much better at giving stuff away than companies trying to make a profit. The government could just take taxes from the rich and pay for everyone's healthcare. It does not have to be that hard. Rich people have enough money and how much money does one person need?

The way it works now is the company that you work for only pays a part of the health insurance cost. This needs to change so the company and the rich owner(s) pay the entire cost. The health insurance gets paid and now you can go to the doctor or hospital. Health insurance premiums can be $1200 to $1500 a month for a family! The doctor should be making house calls for that amount of money. Think of how much doctors and nurses make, and then all of the rich executives in the health insurance company. They should pay higher taxes then we could reduce the cost for the 99% of the people.

Even with health insurance when you go to the doctor you still have to pay deductibles and co-payments so it's not even free after you pay all that insurance. That's why everyone gets rich in the health insurance business. They charge you a lot and they pay out very little. That is why they need to be stopped and the government needs to take it over and make it free!

Big Pharma

When you get sick and need drugs to make you better, why should you have to pay so much for those drugs? The drug company people are rich. We should tax them more and use the money to pay for the drugs for the 99%. They make enough money every year to pay for a lot of other people's drugs. That is what a fair system does. Socialism makes everybody equal and this would not happen in a system like that.

People are dying from cancer and other diseases even though we have the ability to treat so many with drugs if they had the money. People in the 1% can get all the drugs they need. That is why the rich stay in control. They live longer while the poor die more often because they can't get the drugs to stay alive.

Drug companies are making new drugs every day but they are holding them back because they want to make more of a profit. They only want to make the drugs that can make them lots of money like Viagra and drugs for blood pressure. The CEO knows they could cure cancer but then they wouldn't be able to sell all of the other drugs that people use in their cancer treatment.

The drug companies lobby congress to make laws that keep drugs expensive. They want to control the FDA so they can control the market on drugs to keep the prices high. They keep the prices high and make bigger profits meanwhile people die.

The government needs to take over drug companies so we can make them free for people that can't pay. The government could make all the drugs without worrying about making a profit. This would allow them to make the drugs we need instead of making the drugs that make a profit. The government would pay the CEO less or they could tax the executives more to pay for the free drugs.

We need to start thinking about the children and how many we can save with free drugs. We also need to think about all of the old people and how we could keep so many more alive with free drugs. If the government ran the drug companies we could have free drugs for the children and the elderly. That is what we should be doing instead of allowing profits to rule who gets drugs.

The answer is simply to deny profits for Pharmaceutical companies until we can organize a government take-over. How can you trust the private sector to handle something so precious and valuable to our lives?

Big Banks

The big banks are making profits on people that need money. If people need money to start a business; why not lend it to them for free? This way more people can open businesses and have money to share with everyone else. The government is a good example of how this works. When the government runs out of money in the budget they just print more. If the budget for any department in the government is running a deficit they don't just stop doing business they keep going. It hasn't hurt the economy yet.

If the banks gave away more of the money the rich people have invested in those banks, wouldn't that help everyone? If the rich have more than $500,000 in the bank -which is a lot of money in the bank – why not use the money above that to lend to poor people that want to start a business? The rich did not earn that on their own. They used government schools, roads, bridges, and the post office to make their money. So in actuality it is everyone's money.

The banks have trillions of dollars in savings that the rich keep there for retirement. That money could be used to make things fairer for everyone else. How much money do you need in retirement when you already have Social Security? When the rich have accumulated more than $250,000, the rest that they put in should be used to stimulate the economy by lending it to the poor. We can help them start a business or if they are down on their luck and spent all of their other benefits this fund could be a safety net for those that are down on their luck.

The banking industry should be a function of the government and we should limit any profits that can be made on the money they get from rich people. When people put their money in the bank they need to know that they are helping others less fortunate than themselves, and that when they put more than their fair share in the bank it will be used for the less fortunate. That will make the banking system much more responsive to the needs of the people and not just a place for the rich to make more money. This will make the rich feel good too!

The ATM's could have an option for the homeless to get money when they need it. They would have a daily limit but this would cut down on the amount of begging the homeless would have to do on the street corner. There are so many good things you can do with other people's money if you make sure that you don't allow the rich to get richer. The rich get richer on the backs of the poor. This will help build the poor on the backs of the rich.

Subsidies: Why give tax breaks to the rich and business?

The government gives subsidies to farmers, oil companies, banks, and all kinds of other businesses that the rich own. If we didn't give these subsidies we would have a lot more money to balance the budget and give more money to the people that need it.

The government gives tax breaks to farmers of over $250,000,000,000 Billion that could be used for other purposes. The farmers are going to plant crops anyway. So why give them incentives when they are rich anyway? It's not like they will stop planting crops if they don't get the subsidies. We will never run out of food because we are the biggest food producer in the world. If we stopped producing food nobody would eat and we aren't going to do that. If that happened we could have the government grow food instead.

Farmers own a lot of land which makes them rich. If the poor had as much land as Farmer's did they would be rich too. Making a profit on feeding people is like charging too much for healthcare. Everyone has a right to eat. If they don't eat the can die. So how can we allow the government to give tax incentives to the rich farm owners that feed the world? It is almost as if they have a monopoly on the food market and should be stopped.

Oil producers get tax subsidies as well. Look at the ethanol subsidies. We give subsidies to oil companies to use corn in their gas refinement and then we subsidize the farmers that grow the corn. It's the rich feeding the rich. This is how the game gets played in the capitalist system. The rich keep getting richer and the poor keep getting poorer. Why would the rich need all of these subsidies from government? We could use all of that money to pay teachers and build better schools. We should be subsidizing education and using the tax dollars from the rich to pay the teachers more which will make kids smarter.

The government subsidizes exports, housing, healthcare, and many other activities it wants businesses to do. Why not just tax the businesses or take them over so you don't have to give any taxes to the rich?

Subsidies are usually given to get businesses to behave in a certain way. If you just tax them and take away the money to begin with you don't have to ask them to do anything, the government can do it for itself.

Regulations protect the poor!

The Tea Party wants to stop government regulations but who then will protect the poor? Take the taxi industry for example. If the government didn't regulate the taxi industry how safe do you think the taxi cabs would be? That is why it is so expensive to get a medallion in New York to start a taxi company. You need a lot of money to start a taxi company and many rich people do. So if rich people could make more money wouldn't they? They would cut back on safety and hire just anyone off the streets to drive. This would be a safety hazard for the public and the poor.

The fares are regulated so the rich owners don't over charge the unaware consumer that might get ripped off by the rich. If there were no regulations almost anyone could start a taxi company. Anyone with a car and a license could start charging people for a ride. What would that do for the poor? Yeah some might start their own company but there would be too many poor people getting ripped off with high fares.

The government regulates the oil companies to make sure they don't harm the environment. The government regulates the healthcare industry to protect patient rights. The government regulates the airline industry to make sure they are complying with the passenger's rights and safety. The government regulates the food industry so we have safe food to eat. The government regulates the television and radio industry to make sure we hear the right types of programs and our children don't hear the wrong messages and vulgarity. The government regulates the internet to make sure everyone has equal access to the information super highway. The government regulates how much water we use to flush our toilets. The government regulates our lightbulbs to make sure we are saving energy.

The government regulates almost everyone and everything and it is only getting better and we need more regulation. If we don't regulate then the rich will just get richer by making up their own rules. If we want to keep everyone safe and have a fairer society we have to pay for all of these regulators. The best way to do that is to tax the rich and their companies to pay for it since they are the reason we need so many regulations. The Tea Party also talks about how the constitution limits the power of the government to regulate our lives. That is not true because the constitution is a living document and that is why we need to regulate the rich even more.

Big Government

Big government is our friend. It is the only way to level the playing field between the rich and the poor. We use the government to tax the rich so without the government how would we pay for everything we need to give to the working man, working poor, and those down on their luck in society? If we didn't have such a big government and growing, how could we stop the inequity we are seeing today? Who would be looking out for the little guy? Who would our most vulnerable turn to in their time of need?

Without big government to tax the rich we might find scenarios like people having to fend for themselves. If the government was not there to feed the poor the poor might need to work at a job they are over qualified for just to put food on the table! Think about the blow to their pride! Is it fair to count on just churches and non-profit organizations to take care of their neighbors in need? Who would make sure that everyone had all of the needs not just the basic needs of food, shelter, and clothing?

How could we take care of all of the people that come across our borders to do the work no American will do? Who I ask you? The government.

If the people were left to create their own living they would definitely have to work for wages decided by the rich. People with no skills might have to take a minimum wage job and how could they raise a family on that wage? The rich would never give anyone a raise if it weren't for big government. That we know is true because every time the government tries to raise the minimum wage the rich republicans fight it.

There are too many important rights that we have as Americans and citizens of the world to leave it up to the people to decide. The government always has the brightest, smartest, and fairest minds to handle such important issues. Think of the rights the government has to protect all the time: The right to healthcare, the right to eat, the right to have a place to live, a right to make a decent wage, a right to an education, and on it goes. Who would be protecting these rights if not for big government?

When 9/11/2001 happened the government took over the safety at our airports. Before then it was private organizations. Today the TSA has grown to thousands upon thousands of agents protecting our air safety. They are men, women, blacks, whites, middle easterners. They are people that reflect the changing population of our country. These men and women take tests and are chosen based on their race, gender and religion without the past discrimination of having to pass physical tests to ensure they could stop a terrorist attack in an airport if one happened. In the past we would have hired only qualified law enforcement officials but not when the big government is in charge instead of private business.

The big government hires to make sure everyone has a chance to be employed no matter what their skills. Go to any government office and look at the individuals there and you will see the diversity that is America. So when you think about a great job program for people that often can't find work elsewhere, think big government. It is not always the fact that you can get a job done that is important, it is more important that America gives everyone a chance. Some need a better chance than others.

In the end Big Government keeps the rich from getting richer and watches out for the small guy. If we put our faith in big government we will see more diversity in the workplace, more rules to make the playing field fair, industries that otherwise couldn't make it in the market thrive under government grants, and if we keep our focus on taxing the top earners in this country that have always had an unfair advantage by working harder and longer than anyone else, we can fix the disparity and make everyone equal again!

Healthcare is a right!

If you get sick you have a right to care. It's in the Declaration of Independence and has been a principle throughout this country's history. We have a right to life, liberty, and the pursuit of happiness. To have life you need healthcare. Case closed. Some people argue that the constitution limits what the government can do but if we think about life being a right, wouldn't healthcare come to mind.

Doctors are rich and nurses and hospital executives are rich as well. Why should they make so much money when some people can't afford healthcare? Shouldn't a doctor be forced to give care to a patient? Shouldn't a hospital be forced to provide the necessary surgery to keep someone alive? Of course they should.

Doctors spend years and years of their lives training to be a doctor. They invest hundreds of thousands of dollars in schooling and put off being able to work for many years. But after that they make a lot of money. If they are going to be a doctor they should know that if someone needs care they will have to care for them no matter what. If they are trained to cure sick people then they should know they will have to care for all of the sick. They can't pick and choose who they care for. It is the right of the sick to get healthcare - so trained doctors and nurses must provide that care even if the patient can't pay for the services.

In order to ensure that doctors and nurses care for the sick people we need the government to mandate that doctors and nurses provide care. If they are going to go into the medical field they will have to do what the government regulations say no matter if they get paid or not. That is only fair because healthcare is a right.

Minimum Wage

Everyone has the right to get paid enough to raise a family if they are willing to go to work. Employees are the reason businesses have employees. Without employees there would be no employees. People that start businesses and become successful are rich. It is only fair that they pay all of their employees enough to raise a family. Even if the business makes less profit that is OK because we need everyone to be able to make more money so we have equality.

The state of Washington has raised the minimum wage to $15.00 an hour. Now that is good but it is only the beginning. Everyone said that the minimum wage hurts businesses. Everyone said if the minimum wage is raised to $15.00 an hour businesses would leave the state. Businesses have started to complain that they can't afford to pay entry level people $15.00 an hour without raising prices drastically on their products and services.

Prices should be capped so that rich employers can't just raise their prices using the excuse of the increase in the minimum wage. We know they are just using the minimum wage as an excuse. The way to keep the minimum wage from increasing the prices of products and services is to cap prices so the rich business owners don't pass on the costs they should be paying out of their profits.

The minimum wage helps increase the wages for everyone. When the minimum wage gets increased it puts pressure on the business owners to increase the wages they pay their employees and that's a good thing. The minimum wage is a good way to tax the rich without impacting the average person. If the business has to increase the wage they pay, and we put a cap on the price the business owner can charge, then they have to take the money out of their profits and that's a good thing.

If employers try to fire or lay people off they should be punished. We may need to tax employers if they reduce jobs based on the rise in the minimum wage. We should make employers prove that they are being impacted by the minimum wage. There should be a federal department that audits small businesses to ensure they are following all the rules. We should have a cabinet position on pay equality and small business compliance.

There is a proposal out there that we need to pay everyone, whether they work or not, by providing a minimum guaranteed salary to help end poverty. If we just take some of the excessive profits that the rich make and pay everyone we could end poverty. There is so much extra money out there being controlled by so few people and that isn't moral or fair. We can end that here in America if we just share the wealth. Don't we learn when we are young that sharing is a good thing? Then why not share all of the wealth instead of allowing just a few to keep it? Isn't that what a government should do when it works for the people?

Why do women make less than men: that's unfair!

The issue of pay equity can only be partially addressed by the minimum wage. Most rich people are men and it is the fundamental reason women make less than men. Why would men pay women the same wage? A lot of men that own businesses don't even believe women should be in the workplace, especially conservative republican men.

So why do woman make less than men? Some say it's because they leave the workforce to raise a family, therefore they fall behind in their skills or fall out of line for promotions. Others say that women choose careers that are more flexible so they can work and raise a family at the same time. And some even say that women already have the hardest career raising children to be successful and good citizens.

I don't see how any of that matters. If a woman has a title that is the same as her male counterpart, she should be paid the same wage. We should force businesses that hire women to pay them exactly the same as every male in the company. This way even if she does leave the workforce to raise a family she can come back and make the same wage as the rest of the men. The rich business owners would just take the additional pay out of the profits.

There are not enough women in engineering. Engineering is one of the highest paid professions and is dominated by males. If we force engineering companies to hire more women then we can start to close the pay gap. We really need to look at the highest paid professions and put women in those industries. The argument that many women don't like engineering can be fixed if we have Daycare Centers start young girls out playing with blocks, and Legos, and erector sets, and take away the dolls so we support them becoming more like men. Men and women are not different. They have simply been raised in a male dominated culture and we can change that through government programs.

We should not stop until every women makes as much as every man, in every industry, at every position in the organization.

Social Justice

How can there be any social justice when we have so much of the wealth in so few hands? How can we allow this gap in wealth to continue? It is immoral to think that somewhere some rich person by some luck of the draw is living in a 10,000 square foot home, and there are homeless. Somewhere some rich person is dining out at a fancy restaurant, eating sushi, drinking fine wine, and leaving food on their plates when there are people starving all around the world.

Some people have had a tough life through no fault of their own. Why should they be punished? When we have all of the overabundance going to so few people, why can't the excess that is going to the rich be re-distributed to the less fortunate? Could it be that the rich are greedy?

Every quarter the big businesses in this country make billions of dollars in profits. Why can't we simply tax the profits and redistribute more to everyone. They can take some of the money going to the shareholders and set up individual accounts for people in need. We can create accounts for them so the taxes on the profits of the corporations can be distributed to the less fortunate.

This country started by stealing from the Indians. We stole land from the French, Spanish, and Mexicans to create the United States. The rich have gotten rich off the injustice of theft and it is time they pay back some of that wealth to atone for their sins.

The Native Americans have lived on Reservations for years and live in squalor. Too many of these Reservations have been under funded by the federal government, and have failed at being successful on their own. It is time to stop the failure of the federal government and the Reservation leadership, and tax the rich that have taken so much from them.

The African American community has lived in city slums for too long. Public education has failed them, local governments have failed them, the welfare and housing subsidies have failed them, and the neighborhoods are being destroyed right before our eyes. We have not taken enough from the rich to make up for all of the ills of slavery. We need a new program that we can fund by taxing the rich that pays every African American a living wage as reparations.

For too long we have allowed a small group of people to gather all of the wealth and keep it. There is no need for any one person to have more than others. If everyone is paid equally, then everyone becomes equal. The success of social justice will be to take as much as we need to make everyone equal. This will eradicate the poor, eliminate the gap, allow everyone to live in dignity, and it all starts with taxing the rich.

Climate Change Deniers: Tax them into submission to fix emissions!

The world is dying and we need to fix it. The world is dying because of the pursuit of profits. Big business has put profits before the environment since the beginning of time. Businesses have been spewing carbon monoxide into the atmosphere and creating a layer of ozone that is warming the earth. If you don't believe the world is getting warmer you are a denier. All of the scientists agree that the climate is changing. We don't have time to spend with these deniers explaining the facts. The facts are irrelevant at this point.

Even though it seems to snow a lot, and Boston had the most snowfall in history, and the Great Lakes are frozen over, that is not important. We are talking about drastic changes in the weather that is causing climate change. When the weather goes from very cold to very hot, it only proves that the climate changes and the rich business owners need to pay to fix it. We need to stop the weather from changing, and the only way to do that is through a government program funded by taxing the rich and businesses that produce carbon monoxide.

We need to listen to Al Gore and create carbon credits. These carbon credits will be doled out by the government to companies based on the amount of carbon or by a distinguished panel of climate experts picked by Al Gore. If they use up these credits they can buy more of them from other businesses that are environmentally friendly or from the government. These credits will be used to fund the effort to stop the weather from changing. If we can stop the weather from changing we will have accomplished our mission.

The government can also expand this to rich individuals. If the rich want to drive fancy cars, boats, planes, and live in huge houses, they can, but they will be forced to buy carbon credits. This will help the climate change less in the long run.

The government should also pass a law that says climate change is real. This way everyone that denies the climate changes can now be punished for denying. This will eliminate our need to stop wasting time on facts and additional science. We know the science will not change unlike our climate.

Education

Education is a right! Every child in America deserves a good education so they can become productive citizens of the United States. Why should only the rich get a good education? The public school system is the best way to make sure all kids get a fair shot at education. Private schools take away from the effectiveness of public schools. That is why the rich should have to send their kids to public school as well. It isn't fair that the rich get to go to better schools.

That's the thing with the rich, they are always trying to get what's best for their kids leaving everyone else in the public schools. That's why we need to get their kids in the public schools so they don't become smarter than the other kids. This way everyone gets a chance and no one has an advantage. That is fair.

We can't allow a voucher system because then everyone would want to go to the better schools and there would be no one left in the failing public schools. This would be especially helpful in the inner cities and poorer neighborhoods where the public schools are really bad because no one wants to teach there. We need to make sure teachers have to work in these schools to make them better.

A hopeful future can only happen when every child has the same opportunity to graduate so they can get a good job. We need to also look at the testing system because it is biased toward poor kids. Only the rich kids pass the tests so that shows that the test is biased toward the rich. If we tie one hand behind the rich kids back and reduce the time they get to take the test maybe the results would be different.

If you can't graduate from High School it is almost guaranteed you will not be successful. Graduation rates in the poorest neighborhoods are abysmal so we have to do something about that. We need to focus on increasing the graduation rate. If the tests are biased toward the rich, and we know that graduating is a key to success, then let's graduate kids with the lower test scores. This way they can go into the world with a diploma and get a job.

Everyone knows that what they are teaching in school is not really needed to get a job anyway. Most of the time people get jobs because they know people, and it's simply a good old boys club. If we can get more kids in the club they will have the opportunity to graduate. If as many poor kids graduated as rich kids we could tighten the gap between rich and poor.

A college educated person is more likely to succeed, make more money than non-college graduates over a lifetime, and are less likely to be unemployed. We need more college graduates. We should tax the rich so they pay for the kids that can't afford it and make the playing field equal. If we can increase the college educated population by 50% we could reduce unemployment by 50%.

Tax The Rich!

The rich should not complain because if we have more
people working then they can afford to buy the products
they sell, and the rich will make more profits, and then we
can tax more profits, and help everyone.

Privilege

Some people don't realize it but they are privileged. Everything in this country is biased toward certain people that have been lucky enough to be a majority in this country. When these privileged people go to a job interview they have an advantage. When a privileged person applies to schools they have an advantage. It is inherent in the system the Founding Fathers created because they were all privileged guys.

This country was built on the back of slaves. They built everything including the roads and bridges we now drive to the supermarket on. So it is only fair that the rich people that got so much from slavery have to pay back into the system.

Privileged people are a majority, and any time you have a majority you have to tax them more to pay for the unfairness they created. Privileged people can never understand the challenges facing minorities and the poor so it is not even worth explaining to them how it works. They keep asking: "how is being privileged an advantage? I grew up poor and my family came from another country way after slavery so how am I privileged?" If they can't figure it out how can we explain it?

The 1%

We can't have a 1% class anymore. We can fix it easily by taxing the 1% so they have the same amount of money as the 99%. All of the wealth is going to the 1%. No matter how bad the economy is the 1% is always getting richer. You have heard the saying "the rich keep getting richer"? That is because they are part of the 1%'rs. They make so much money and then they invest it and create more businesses and make more money. It is a vicious cycle and everyone else is left out. Just because they come up with an idea, finance it, risk everything they have, why should they reap all of the rewards?

The 1% is very powerful and control congress. That is why the laws never change. They are crony capitalists and know how to work the political system. That is why we must tax them so they don't have the money and that will reduce the power they wield.

Why should a CEO make $1,000,000,000 and the janitor only makes $8 an hour? How is that fair? They work in the same company and that janitor works really hard. He/She should get a piece of that money. It shouldn't always go to the top.

Income Inequality

Even if we succeed in getting the minimum wage raised it doesn't address the entire issue of income inequality. Income inequality is a much broader issue that can only be solved by taxing the rich. The fact that some people make a lot of money and others make a lot less is proof there is income inequality.

If the government set wages to be equal people could still go into different careers but they would simply get paid the same amount of money. The wages the government sets would be living wages so that everyone could participate in the American Dream! Just because someone might be more talented than another individual we must make it fair so everyone can make more money!

Let's take an example. The man or woman that works every day picking up the trash for the city or town works really hard. Why should they make less than say, a lawyer? The lawyer works in an office and doesn't have to go out in the elements every day. The lawyer gets to stay inside and work in a nice office. They do spend more time and money going to school but in the end it is better for society if everyone makes the same amount of money. If we can tax the rich to pay for education then the cost of school for the lawyers, doctors, and engineers of the world will not be an issue.

The reason unions have been so effective for the people and a target of the rich is that the union sets wages fairly and they protect people that don't work as hard. Just look at any union and you will see fairness. The business can't just fire someone for being late. They have to go through a process to make sure the employee isn't being unfairly targeted. If it were not for unions many people would have been fired.

The wages unions bargain for give everyone in the union a raise even if the company didn't think they deserved one. If a company doesn't have a union all of the extra money goes into their pockets in profits. Without the workers the company would have no profits to begin with.

How could it hurt the economy to have more people making a lot more money and everyone making a larger but equal salary? More money and more people being able to buy stuff could only make it better for everyone. So if we tax the rich to make more people equal we will have more money being spent by more people. It is a policy the government should enforce to make us all more equal.

Fairness

Overall fairness is something we should strive for in our society. It would be better if life was fair for women, minorities, and all other groups to be equal in every way in our society. It is the role of government to ensure fairness. These programs need to be funded by the people that have benefited from our society for so many years. It is not fair that some people have taken advantage of the system and others have been left on the sidelines.

A tax policy that underwrites the programs that create equality will help everyone take advantage of the American Dream!

Inheritance Tax

Some people have had the advantage of hard working parents. These parents have sacrificed and created large sums of wealth to pass down to their families. This is not fair to the people that don't have parents who created wealth. Why should kids be punished if their parents didn't save for their future? That is why the inheritance tax on the rich is so important.

We need to stop this generational advantage of families that provide these benefits for their families. That is why we need an aggressive tax on the rich so that every American can share in this wealth created by these individuals. Why should the families of the rich be the only ones to take advantage of this wealth creation?

When people die, especially rich people, they should pay back the money they made while they were alive. They have already lived a life that is so unfair compared to the rest of the population. The family of the rich people didn't earn that money so why not tax the inheritance to the fullest. We should eventually end any ability for the rich to pass down their inheritance to their family. But in the meantime we should start with a rate of 90% and increase it gradually until it is finally 100%.

If everybody has the same opportunity to create wealth then the families of the rich will have the opportunity to be rich but not because they were fortunate enough to have successful parents. That is like winning the lottery.

It is time to tax away any wealth created and give it back to the American people!

How much is enough?

CEO's in this country make too much money. How can a country that prides itself on fairness allow a CEO to make $10 Million a year and a janitor at the same company make $8.00 an hour? This goes against the American Dream. How can a janitor achieve the American Dream making $8 an hour?

If someone makes a $1,000,000 a year isn't that enough? The arguments of fairness, equality, and equal outcome are easy to make when you have a country that is so rich. The founders talked about equality for all and were against the King and Monarchy so that every individual would have a fair shot in America. That is why this country is a "shining city on a hill"! We need to give people a chance to participate in the American Dream by taxing the rich and spreading that wealth to all Americans.

There are people in this country that own 2, 3, and 4 homes. The rich sometimes own even more. How can a fair government allow that to happen? How can we the American people allow such inequality to thrive and prosper?

Most Americans will agree with policies that allow the rich to keep some money but puts a limit on their wealth accumulation. We can debate the amount that is enough but we need to do it now. Poverty has been growing over the past 8 years and it is urgent that we don't lose another generation to poverty.

Rich Hand

The rich often donate to the poor for tax purposes but we need to make their giving mandatory. That is the role of the Federal Government. The next democratic presidential candidate should put together a platform to address this issue. It is a winning message.

You didn't build that!

You often hear the argument from very successful people that they created their wealth on their own through sweat and determination. But how could they have built a business if the roads, bridges, schools, and opportunities were not already there for them? These things were built by the government. Without the government infrastructure and the schools that gave them the knowledge to be successful, how could they have built their business?

When individual citizens succeed is it not a valid expectation that they give back? And if they are really successful shouldn't they give more back based on the success they have had? The rich don't acknowledge that without the government they could not have succeeded. We need to set limits on the wealth so that people know at the beginning they will be taxed according to their level of success. Why should individuals that have not had the same success be punished? If we make the system more equal everyone can prosper - not just the people that succeed. We are all Americans after all.

In the 2008 presidential campaign, now President Obama, had an exchange with a plumber on the campaign trail. The plumber was upset about the high tax burden on his small plumbing business. The president said to the plumber that he "didn't build that" on his own. He suggested that government played a role in his success and it caused an uproar in the country. It made it very clear that people need to be educated about the role the government has played in this country's success.

Hillary Clinton, a presidential candidate again in 2016 has talked about how businesses don't produce profits. Profits are enabled by government. She is a strong advocate for wealth equality. She understands that we need to equalize outcomes in this country for the less fortunate. This will make for a just and moral country.

What Equality Means

The fact that we are born into different circumstances should not mean that every American shouldn't have the same experience in this wealthy country. Some people are going to make more money than others but money should not be the way we measure success. We need every American to be successful and that means some people will have to give more than others.

How can we as Americans accept inequality? How can such a rich country allow some to live in squalor and others live in paradise on earth? It is a conclusion no thinking person can accept as an outcome we can live with. We are better than that and the best way to make things equal is to tax the rich. They can afford it first of all but more importantly we need to give everyone the right to the American Dream.

It is time to end the debate and start to take action. The action is to have the federal government control the flow of wealth in this country. We need to come together and agree that the wealth created is not the individual's wealth but rather the government's wealth. If we move from individual wealth to communal wealth we will be better off as a society. If people don't agree, like denying Global Warming, the deniers must be ostracized.

The presidential candidate that takes up this mantra of taxing the rich will reap the reward through votes in the upcoming 2016 election. The country is ready to become what the founders always wanted it to be: equal. It is time to realize their dream for the America they founded.

Conclusion

If you believe the way to create wealth for everyone is to tax the rich then you need to vote democrat in this upcoming election. This election could be the turning point for this country where we finally make the tax system fair for all. The gap between the richest people and the poorest people has been growing and it is time to stop it, finally.

The wealth of America needs to be distributed more equally and the federal government is the best way to achieve equal distribution to all. We as Americans have been given an opportunity to finally show the world how a government can create opportunity for all. We should be an example for everyone that believes that equality is a worthy cause. If you want to make it a reality vote democrat.

The Argument

I wrote this book to point out the way we look at political arguments today. Today's arguments are emotional arguments not fact based arguments. Emotion is so much easier than actually thinking through and analyzing results of the impact of politics on people's lives. To prove my point, ask any person on the street if the Constitution is a living document. Most people think it is but that is not logical. If the constitution is a living document then that means it can change. The constitution doesn't change, circumstances change.

Walter Williams, a black professor at George Mason University says it best: "if we were to play poker and the rules were living, and I could change the rules at any time during the game, would you play poker with me? If you would then I would love to play poker with you!" The point being that the rules cannot be changed in the middle of a game or they are not rules. The rules lay the foundation for the game. The constitution is the foundation of our civil society and it was designed to limit what the federal government could do and most importantly to protect individual liberty. The key word being "individual". It does not say it protects the "collective" liberty. It does that only by placing the sole emphasis on the individual. Otherwise a group could vote to take away liberties from individuals with no recourse.

When I was writing as a liberal making the arguments that they do it was actually quite easy and I felt unencumbered to any logic. It was like a blank page and I could write any words I wanted to without consequence or fear of needing to support my arguments. I could simply write what I felt. Feelings are not what made this country great. Don't get me wrong, feelings are important and play a role in life, but not in deciding public policy at the federal level.

If you were reading this book up to this point and your blood was boiling or you were scratching your head, you have solid political instincts. If you were reading this book to this point and you agreed and perhaps were cheering me on, you need to reestablish your knowledge of the founding of this nation, human behavior, and the results of your instincts to tax the rich as the answer to any political problem we face.

I am going to take a moment and add some analysis to some of the concepts I have argued as a leftist. And I do believe people that support the concept of taxing the rich are leftist and not traditional democrats. I also believe that people who support taxing the rich are not thinking through the ramifications of what they are supporting. I believe if most people think through to the logical conclusion of taxing the rich they would change their position.

Human Behavior

The study of human behavior is the foundation Thomas Jefferson and many of the founders based the US Constitution's principles and greatest protections on. The study of human behavior reveals that the basic instincts humans have must be addressed in order to have a civil and productive society. The reason the United States has been such a miracle in history is because the constitution was framed with human behavior at the forefront of consideration in limiting the federal government. The founders knew human behavior is flawed and protections against the propensity of governments to infringe on basic human rights had to be neutralized.

Jefferson and many founders studied the past civilizations and were committed to finding a system that would not fail like all others did. This study of past civilizations revealed that the only way to have a sustainable society was to focus on the individual, protect the individual from the group (faction), and to base the society in a moral foundation. To think about what they accomplished is nothing short of a miracle. The reason we as Americans have experienced such wealth and prosperity is not just happenstance. It is not a mistake but by design. That design is the constitution's protection of the individual and limits it placed on the federal government.

Knowing how human behavior works does not take a degree from Harvard or any other institute of higher learning. It simply takes the ability to observe and be honest about the conclusions you come to based on these observations. For example, when you have observed any meeting of a group of people, say a school board meeting, and someone stands up and offers a different opinion from the majority, what happens? That person is vilified, booed, and felt to be a threat to the overall group. Depending on how emotional the subject of the meeting is, it can become borderline violent. The founders knew that individuals had to be protected from the group. Here is a simpler example: Two wolves and a sheep are deciding on what to have for lunch, would a democracy be a good system to protect all three at the lunch gathering?

Our system is not a pure democracy. It is a constitutional republic that slows down the emotional aspect inherent in democracies. The republic is more deliberate and protects individuals from being harmed by majorities simply by taking a vote. I will not go deep into the functions of a republic vs. democracy but the point being our system protects smaller groups from being ravaged by larger groups. It is what has kept the "rich" from being voted out of their wealth. So far it has been effective in protecting people's wealth. It is one of the reasons the left despises the constitution. It stops them from simply forming a majority to steal the wealth created by individuals. It is the same as two wolves and a sheep voting on what to have for lunch.

Emotions are so much easier to cultivate than making the difficult arguments. So many emotional arguments appeal to our human nature. We want to help people and when we see few with a lot, and many with less, it seems "right" to "spread the wealth." But actually the exact opposite is what drives the more productive behavior from humans. Fear and need can be excellent drivers for individuals to become more productive. Expecting people to take care of themselves drives better behaviors than giving people what they need without any effort. The later drives entitlement.

Social Circumstances

The argument used to sell the idea of taxing the rich is that some people just have an unfair advantage over others. There is this new concept of "privilege" that is a cancer to our nation's founding principles. There is no privilege, only hard work and determination that impact outcomes. To suggest someone's background will decide their success or give them an advantage is illogical. There are examples everywhere of people coming to this country, working hard, and succeeding from every race, gender and ethnic background. The American Black community needs to embrace this now and stop waiting for politicians to wave some magic "fairness" wand to help them succeed. There are arguments made that growing up in single parent households, poor communities with lousy schools, and a host of other circumstances cannot be overcome to be successful in this country. That is a self-fulfilling prophesy if accepted by any individual. The real answer is hard work and determination. The left's answer is that the government must re-distribute the wealth of the fortunate few; and this must be rejected by individuals if they want to be successful.

The idea that in America we can't overcome our social circumstances is a cancer that undermines the spirit of the individual. Every American has a story that could be used as an excuse. Many Americans born into wealth have died in poverty. The promise of America is if you work hard, start a business, or come up with an idea you can become wealthy beyond your wildest dreams. That promise has been the fuel to propel this nation to a status never before seen by human society. The idea that the wealth created by these dreamers should be a target for the government is the same as killing the goose that lays the golden eggs.

When people are born into poverty here in America, they are given opportunities not found anywhere else in the world. Access to education to build the knowledge necessary to be successful is not dependent on what your family's current level of financial success is or where they are from. Unlike many countries where being born into poverty is a sentence to a life of poverty, here in the US it can be the inspiration needed to try harder to make a better life for yourself. The "American Dream" is built on the idea that anyone can make it here. It is why people risk everything to come here. The people that most often appreciate the dream are people that have come to this country, first generation.

If we think about the argument that some people need to be given things because they can't do it themselves, it is actually an insult to their being. In the inner cities, where many poor are Black and Hispanic, the assumption that these individuals can't be successful on their own is the ultimate insult. It has become a prison in these communities precisely because this idea of inferiority has been accepted by some in our society. The idea that taxing and taking from some successful person to hand out to someone in these communities as the "fix" to poverty is criminal. It is criminal because we are taking one person's property, and the other person's dignity.

The "fix" is a change in policy and attitude that makes the assumption we are all capable of greatness and success. Fear is the mother of invention, and people need to invent themselves into productive members of society. By giving people the property of others we are promoting weakness, humiliation, envy, and destroying the drive and incentive of generations of individuals.

If the idea that if you are poor you can't change your circumstances so you must be helped by the government was true, how can we account for all of the successful people that started with nothing and became successful? There is case after case of poor Black, White, Hispanic, Asians, and any every other group you care to name of people becoming rich from their ideas, talents, and hard work.

Taxing the rich makes no sense if we want the poor to have a successful life because many of the rich were the poor. The rich to poor and poor to rich "highway" is a constantly changing group of people traveling back and forth. People create successful businesses that go bankrupt. People come across hard times and loose it all and have to start over again. People that are poor today can be the rich next week. It is the driver and incentive to try our best and once we have achieved success to hang on to it for dear life.

The government has no claim to the hard work of individuals. If the government was in charge of making people want to work hard our country would have collapsed a long time ago. The will to succeed has many hurdles but in the end there is no permanent barrier that can't be overcome in this country.

Fairness

What is fair? We are taught our entire life that we must treat everyone fairly. But how can that be? If someone is attempting to rob my home or harm my family, should I treat them fairly or take action to protect my family? We all want to be treated the way we treat others. Unless of course they treat us in a way we don't want to be treated.

Fair is also a "relative" term not an "absolute" term. Fair can be interpreted differently depending on your perspective on life and the way you were raised. In comparison to an absolute term that has one definition for all - like being treated as equals. Being equal means we are all treated the same. There is no room for interpretation when we say that we are going to treat everyone equally.

So if we want to treat everyone equally, how do you exclude the rich when it comes to taxation? Compared to if you want to tax people fairly, who decides what fair is? I think it is fair that everyone is taxed at the same rate. People on the left believe that taxing the rich at a higher rate is fair because they have more. So there is a discrepancy between how people interpret the definition of fair. Not so with equal. That is why we need to reference the constitution when it comes to treating individuals equally. The argument to tax the rich people at a higher rate falls apart when we treat people equally rather than fairly.

Take a moment to put yourself in the shoes of someone who is "rich". If you happen to open a restaurant, work for years to make it successful, and a company comes along that believes it would make a great franchise, and you risk it all on the idea your idea could be duplicated throughout the country, and you make a lot of money, you should be proud of what you accomplished, right? After all of your years of sacrificing family time, vacations, personal time, holidays, kid's events, and all of the things employees get to do, you finally have earned your opportunity. Then someone comes along to claim a piece of your success, complain you have too much, and insult you that "you didn't build that", do you think you would agree that taxing the "rich" is fair? It is anything but fair. Actually it is the definition of being treated unfairly.

The argument the left makes to "tax the rich" is not based on solid ground. It is built on quicksand, and if we agree with the premise of "fairness" we move forward at the country's peril. If we succeed in taking more and more from the "rich" or people that are more successful than others, we undermine the incentive and drive by individuals to take risks and work harder. If the government is allowed to take the majority of wealth from successful individuals to transfer to other people, why create more wealth? For example, imagine going to work every day, working hard, spending 10 to 12 hours a day, and when you get your check you have to give 75% of the check to people that don't work. Your $750.00 paycheck is reduced to $199 dollars after giving 75% to the government. Would you consider that fair? I think most of us would not.

It does not matter how much you make, if you take 75% of

anyone's wealth, you will reduce their willingness to create that wealth. If we apply these larger concepts of taxation to real people like ourselves, it changes the perspective. But too many people don't apply that logic to the people who have made what they consider a lot of money. A lot of money is a relative term and means different things to different people. That is why we need to think in terms of equal. Equal protection under the law. Equal % taxation for all individuals.

Taxing the "rich" at the same rate as everyone else will still result in more money coming from the "rich". That is the foundation of a flat rate tax by the federal government. It is simple math. If I make $30,000 a year and get taxed 10%, I pay $3000 in taxes. If I make $100,000 and get taxed 10%, I pay $10,000 in taxes. If I make $3,000,000 a year and get taxed 10%, I pay $30,000 in taxes. The example proves that the more money you make, the more money you pay in taxes. This is an equitable system that is fair (in my opinion), but it will never satisfy the left's argument for taxing the rich. They want to punish success, not tax people equally.

So the next time you hear the argument we need to tax the rich more, ask yourself: "what do you mean?" Define what you hope to do by taxing the rich more?

Equal Pay

We are about to make an argument that will need us to think deeper and check our emotions at the door. When I discussed the need to think in equal rather than fair, I am about to throw a wrench into the brain waves and say equal pay is almost impossible. When we talk about taxing people fairly we must think equal, when we talk about paying people, equal is not the benchmark. In the first example we are talking about government taking people's money, in the later we are talking about private business owners paying a wage based on value.

It is not easy to be a thinking person. We must go deeper than emotion. When we talk about the difference between more conservative thinking and the left, it is simply taking the time to break down the argument. When we talk about government taking our private property (taxes), and business owners paying their employees for the work they produce (wages), equality cannot be the benchmark.

In the system that has provided us and the world with the greatest wealth and opportunity, there is a basic need to understand that paying a wage can rarely be equal if we want to be fair. In the private sector some people just work harder and are more valuable than others. There are rare cases where two people perform the same task and can be measured equally. But as happens most in a capitalist economic system - that is the exception rather than the rule. Especially in today's more information/intellectual based economy. The fact that people believe if they work harder than the next guy then they can get ahead is an economic driver for our country. If the idea of getting ahead was taken away with some form of equality, it would represent doom for our economic system.

I will address the capitalist system in the next section. What I hope you will think about here is the way we think about the argument and that words mean things. Emotions are real but they cloud the real arguments.

As we discussed the minimum wage, the same principle applies. Taking a number randomly to determine what someone should be paid is unfair. A business owner cannot survive if some entity from outside his business decides what he/she has to pay the employee. There has been a push by groups recently to raise the minimum wage in the fast food industry to $15 an hour. First question you should ask is: why $15 an hour and not $50 an hour? If the person answering the question says that would be too much, the next question is: why is $50 too much?

The reality is that these people know that wages must be tied to productivity. What the left is doing when it is promoting $15 is to create a political issue. They don't care how much these people make, they just want to attract people to vote for their cause so they can continue to wound our capitalist system. They want to wound and destroy a system they believe is unfair. But if you think about capitalism from an objective perspective and not let emotion drive your thinking, capitalism is the fairest system ever created. Capitalism rewards hard work, ingenuity, and risk.

The results of randomly raising the minimum wage is destroying jobs in the states and cities where they are being implemented. The only people a raise in the minimum wage helps is the people using it as a political tool. The people that at one point may have been considered a potential employee, now become too expensive to hire. The people that received the increase to $15 an hour now have to work even harder because the company can't afford to hire more people to do the work.

In business there are hard and fast economic laws. They are called laws because there are no exceptions and apply to the situation every time. The law of supply and demand creates price fluctuations in relation to the necessity of the product or service. Let's look at gasoline for your car. When the supply of gas increases because people reduce the amount they drive, prices fall. When the supply of gas is reduced to some event like a refinery shutdown; demand increases and prices rise.

When you increase the price (wage) of an employee to a business, it reduces the demand for the employee. It also increases the likelihood of the employer finding a cheaper alternative like automation. We have seen it in every automobile factory. The cost of labor (wages) increased to a point that replacing humans with machines was less costly to the company than hiring humans. Every action has an equal and opposite reaction. That is a law in physics but it also applies in economics.

Capitalism vs. Socialism

It sounds wonderful to say everyone is equal. But in reality we are not. Some people are more driven than others. Some people find math really easy. Some people have instincts about others that are almost clairvoyant. The fact is we have different skills and different abilities. To make the assumption that everyone is equal is to defy the laws of nature. That is not to say that everyone in a society should not be given an equal chance to succeed. This is where people get confused. They get confused between equal opportunity and equal outcomes. Equal opportunities good, equal outcomes bad.

Capitalism has been the engine of this country's wealth. There is no denying that the reason America is economically head and shoulders amongst the world is capitalism. We encourage people to be all they can be and if they succeed they get to keep their rewards. It is the goose that lays all of the golden eggs. This is not a hard concept to understand. All you have to do is apply it to any situation in your life.

If you have spent your life trying to do the right things like get an education, work hard at every job that you have ever had, learned new skills at the jobs you have had, or given it your best at anything you have done, you are most likely living the American Dream. The "American Dream" is not about what you have achieved, it is what you have had the opportunity to obtain if you work hard. There are no guarantees given in the pursuit of the American Dream, only the chance that if you work hard, try to do the right things you may be rewarded.

You see, in most of the world, governments are there to suppress the people. In America we control the government. The government is of the people, by the people, for the people. This is unique in the world and we often forget this because we are so blessed. We often project our circumstances on others throughout the world. This is a mistake we make at our own peril. To assume that others believe the way we do is to make mistakes in how we approach policies. Capitalism is an economic bi-product of freedom and our constitution. The reason there is so much conflict between people that support socialism and those that support capitalism is that freedom cannot be maintained in a socialist system. In order for socialism to work you must force people to give up their wealth to give to others. That is not freedom that is tyranny.

When you force people to give up the rewards of their work, the people that create the wealth quickly conclude that any efforts to be more successful are taken for the betterment of everyone. Initiative is squashed so wealth is the casualty. When people are free and can keep the rewards of their hard work they work harder and initiative is nourished. This creates more incentive and more wealth. The creation of wealth and allowing people to keep their wealth spawns altruism and charity to support the less fortunate in society. If you take people's wealth they are less likely to donate to charity because they have had their wealth confiscated and expect the government to take care of the less fortunate.

Capitalism does not favor the rich, it creates the rich. The argument that only the rich benefit from capitalism is backwards. You can only become rich if you participate in capitalism. The argument should be how we create more rich people, not how we should punish them. If we focus on nourishing the environment that creates wealth instead of stirring up envy for those that have been successful - we would see even more people in the "rich" category. We should be looking at increasing the 1% to the 100%.

If we think logically about focusing our efforts on taxing the rich we will destroy the rich. That is exactly what the history of socialism has taught us; socialism destroys wealth. The only wealth is confiscated by an elite class of people and the 1% goes from people that earned it to those that stole it. Why would we support a system that has a history of destroying everything the American Dream was built upon? Why would we demonize success? Why wouldn't we support the system that has bucked history's trend of poverty and limited opportunity for the common man?

The Impact of Profits

Profits are simply a reflection of success and the product of hard work appreciated by a market place. For example, if you start a restaurant and people enjoy your food and are willing to pay you a fair price, come to your restaurant on a regular basis, tell others about it so your clientele grows, and the costs to run the restaurant are kept to an acceptable level, there may be a few dollars left over which is called a profit. Profits have been demonized for some reason but they are simply an indicator of a successful business. If there are no profits there is no business.

So if you want to tax the rich they need to have profits to tax. The policies that government should pursue is to improve all business profits. The more profits the larger the tax revenue. If the left was truly concerned about more tax revenue to help people they would embrace profits.

Profits can be as little as $1 to billions of dollars. Profits are not something to be targeted. Profits should be celebrated because the more profit a company has the more likely that company is creating jobs for other people to make money and pay taxes. At some point, and this point is different for everyone depending on their definition of success, profits create a sense of philanthropy in people to give back to the less fortunate. To conclude there should be a limit on profits is to not understand the good that profits support. Any charity will tell you that people who make a profit are more likely to help others. The greater the profits the greater the giving.

If the government targets profits to give to others it only creates resentment. The reason resentment is created is because the recipients of government confiscation of wealth are not particularly deserving, they are simply chosen for a political reason. When people give from their profits out of the goodness of their hearts, they have control and support people truly deserving. People giving to charity from their own profits give based on research and intrinsically good reasons. Not political reasons.

Taxing the rich sounds good until you find out who the left considers rich. You might be surprised what "rich" means to some. Especially people in politics that have an interest in creating favor with a particular group. A politician representing a group of citizens that have an average income of $20,000 per year would see people that make $80,000 per year as rich compared to their group. The point being that profits and being "rich" is relative to where you find yourself on the economic ladder.

Profits are the fertilizer for any economic garden to grow. America is a garden that is envied around the world because we have had endless fertilizer to nurture our economic garden. If you target the fertilizer for extinction the garden dies. As a nation we have always celebrated people that have realized profits beyond their wildest dreams. We should celebrate profits and ignore the envy that is being cultivated by the left.

Targeting "Big" Companies

The trick to creating envy and demonizing capitalism is to call something big. Big Oil, Big Pharma, Big Banks, etc. It is an effort to take any personal connection out of the equation. If it is a big company it doesn't care what it does to the people, environment, or the less fortunate. The funny thing is that these same people arguing about the evil of big business are the same people that promote big government.

The bigger any organization is the less personal it becomes. It is a "law" of nature. Every organization starts with a small group of people with a core belief and as it grows the further the people drift from the original mission. This is true in both business and government. Our country was created by a small group of founders and as it has grown it has drifted from the original intent. Microsoft, HP, Google, Facebook all started in garages and dorm rooms. Many companies can claim the same roots but the point is that when any group grows it tends to lose its core mission and evolves.

The targeting of big companies becomes an easy target for those intent on taxing the rich. Why would the average individual care if some "big" organization gets taxed more? If your neighbor was targeted to be taxed more there might be some outrage. But tell someone you're going to tax some big entity and they could care less, and in many cases have no issue supporting the concept. Until they see how it impacts them directly.

Big companies become big because they sell stock to people that are willing to risk their money to help that company grow in return for a profit on the money they lend in the form of stock. In reality "big" companies are really just a lot of individual people holding stock in the company. Even big "institutional" investors are simply people that represent individuals in a mutual fund, union, or other organized group of individual investors. In reality there is no such thing as a big company. When you tax a big company you are simply taxing a large group of individuals.

The reason there is not a lot of push back is that most people don't make the connection that their 401K is the big company. There are many reasons for this but mostly it is finances and politics don't interest most Americans. Big mistake.

The profits of big companies go to millions of Americans in the form of dividends reinvested in 401K and pension plans. How else would people be able to retire after 30 years without investments they have making a profit? The next time you hear the mantra to tax "Big Company X", remember it is your retirement they are targeting to take to give to someone else.

CEO's and executives at "big" companies do make big money but so do people in big government. The pension plans and pay for politicians are much larger in reality in government than the private sector. Government employees and politicians have no accountability so if they fail they get a salary and pension no matter what they do.

The private sector pays more money but their success is dependent on being successful. In reality the private sector big executive could lose it all.

Big companies also give significant amounts of money to charity and create a huge tax base by employing a lot of people. So why target them? Why not support policies that help all companies to become big?

At some point all taxing the big rich corporations does is reduce employment, charitable giving, and reduce the size of the big corporation. Could it be that the true goal of taxing big corporations is to simply put them out of business? The question then becomes, is that good policy? Would we be better off without Apple, Microsoft, Google, Shell, US Bank, Ford, and hundreds of other successful companies? Can we tax them to a point that it no longer makes sense to have a presence in the United States? We already have and that's a book that has already been written.

The alternative to our private sector businesses is the government running essential organizations like agriculture, manufacturing, healthcare, and every other business. If we take an honest look at the healthcare takeover to date, it is a disaster. If you look closely at health insurance the new regulations have essentially ended coverage. Most plans have $6,000 - $13,000 deductibles before insurance kicks in. The exception is preventative check-ups and a few other basic services that are low cost and could be paid for directly out of pocket. What we effectively have now is very expensive catastrophic insurance plan and we pay for most other services. Insurance simply protects any wealth we have created; home, savings, retirement, from being confiscated for healthcare bills.

Can you imagine any industry being run by the government that would not fail? It is often said" if the federal government was in charge of the Sahara Desert, it wouldn't be long before there was a shortage of sand." Anything big government touches turns rotten. There are degrees of rotten but it is all rotten.

Minimum Wage

The argument for increasing the minimum wage is a very appealing one when you simply think about giving people more money for their work. Most people do not think about it any deeper than the emotional lure, and the casual observer of politics or economics can be easily convinced to support the appeal to force the "rich" business owner to pay his/her people more.

The media has done all of the groundwork for this argument by demonizing the wealthy business owner as being greedy and selfish. The media focuses on the "rich" and all of their luxuries but fail to tell the stories of failure and losses that are often part of the journey to becoming successful. When someone like Steve Jobs, Bill Gates, Ray Crock, or other successful entrepreneurs are highlighted in the media, they focus on the amount of money they are making and not the hard work and sacrifice it took to get there.

We used to encourage and dream about emulating these successful people but now we teach our kids that this type of "inequality" is a bad thing. But it is not a bad thing if wealth is earned legally and not by gaming the political system.

CEO's, executives, and owners make a lot more than the front line entry level employee. There is nothing inherently wrong with some people making more than others. Wages are a reflection of the value a position in a company brings to the organization. The owner that sacrificed, invested their time and money to create and develop the business deserves every penny they determine is fair compensation for their efforts. No government should have a say in an individual's compensation. They often take $1 when times are tough, or no salary at all when the business struggles, but you rarely hear about the difficult times.

When the owner or business set the wages for their jobs, they are a product of the nature of the work; how much training and education is needed, how much return a job well done has on the company's bottom line, and the market conditions of the labor market. For example, the job of a front line worker in the fast food industry takes little education, and can be done by almost anyone. So competition for that job in the labor market is high. Because there are millions of people that can do that job the cost of labor for the employer is low. It is an entry level job that any High School student can do and therefore does not command a high wage. On the other hand and engineer that designs and builds the locations for the fast food company commands a higher wage. Engineers go to college and spend a lot of time maintaining their skills. They need to be good at math and understand architectural plans. This is not an entry level job.

If you simply tax the "rich" owner by forcing him/her to pay an increased minimum wage, you reduce the money available for more productive investment by the company. This reduces jobs by limiting expansion and investment in the business. If forcing the "rich" to pay higher wages improved the economy as suggested, why is the economy in

Seattle struggling since they raised the minimum wage to $15? The "rich" are not struggling because of the increased wage, it is the people looking for their first job or have limited skills who are suffering.

If you tax something you get less of it. Think about your economic behavior to prove the point. Say you want to rent a car for your next vacation. You search for cars and you see prices of $33 a day to $57 a day. You are staying for 5 days so you calculate the cost to be $165.00 for the week. This price seems to be reasonable. Then you dig a little deeper and you find out that rental cars are taxed at a very high rate. After taxes the actual daily rate is $51 a day. The rate is now $255.00 for the week. Would that tax rate impact your decision? At the least you have to think harder about the purchase, but many people decide not to rent cars at all because of the cost. The consideration of the tax rate when purchasing airlines tickets, hotel rooms, cigarettes, a home in a particular state and county, and thousands of other transactions can determine if we buy. The additional costs of taxation impact financial decisions every day.

Taxes raise prices, higher prices reduce purchases, and limit the goods sold. The same happens when you force employers with a tax (minimum wage) to pay higher wages. You get less job creation because taxes make the jobs more expensive. Taxing the "rich" owners of businesses actually hurts everyone except the rich.

Conclusion

The next President of the United States, Congressional candidate, Senate candidate, or any political candidate need to understand the impacts of taxing the rich. Not only taxing the rich, but demonizing the rich. It is bad policy. It may be "good" politics to get elected but it is really bad policy for the country if we want to remain healthy, wealthy, and free.

The question we have to answer if we want to improve the prospects for a brighter future is: why do so many people support political arguments that hurt so many people and jeopardize the future of this country? There are many answers but I believe most people treat political arguments much like they support their favorite sports team. People will support their favorite sports team because they have an emotional connection with that team. Party politics works in a similar way. The political party is our "team", and we will support our team with an almost "knee jerk" reaction. We take little time to think and apply mostly emotions.

If you knew that supporting government entitlement programs hurts people, would you still support the programs? If you knew that raising the minimum wage reduces the number of jobs for entry level employees would you still support raising the wage? If you know that taking money from someone is wrong, and the government takes more money from some because they worked harder and made more, would you still support taking that money? If you knew charities would receive less money from people if we raise taxes on the rich, would you still support higher taxes on the rich? If you know that by reducing taxes on the rich and everyone else as a matter of fact, more money is collected for government programs, would you still be against reducing taxes?

We need to think, not feel our way through political issues. We need to stop falling prey to arguments designed to pull on our emotional heart strings and analyze the actual results of the arguments being made. We would never just accept what a salesman claims in our daily lives without walking through in our mind the claim he/she is making, would we?

The country is at a turning point and needs more thinkers. Our schools have undermined the foundation of our nation. The left has taken a foothold in our education and media industries and has reduced the knowledge needed to maintain our system of government. Our citizens have been dumbed down in civics education, basic economics, and the study of history. Especially human behavior and the results of systems like communism and socialism.

The left has demonized capitalism, success built on hard work, and traditional values that have made the country strong. They have replaced inspiration with dependence and have turned our nation's youth against the founding principles of this country. Is this to argue that our system is perfect? Absolutely not, but there is no greater beacon of freedom and opportunity than what we have in this country. There is no reason we should feel guilt or shame. We have a system that encourages a constant evaluation of our principles.

We have conquered slavery, we celebrate people based on their achievements and behaviors, and we are the only country to still inspire hope for a better future. The country is literally being invaded by people that want a better life. We need to evaluate each and every one of them to ensure they are coming to this country for the right reasons.

The left has segmented us into groups so they can divide us and conquer the spirit of individualism that has fueled the greatness we enjoy. The founders were brilliant and not just a bunch of "old white guys" out of touch with today's society. They were actually the reason the world is a better place because they laid the groundwork and framework for our country to deliberately become better. Without the system they devised, a Constitutional Republic, the world would be a much different place. The system celebrates us as individuals not by groups. The individual is the key to ending all discrimination. There are no groups in this country that shouldn't be able to overcome any biases if they focus on their own individual achievement.

The left wants us to fight amongst ourselves so they can control the system and change it. The people on the left today have dangerous intentions. They reject your ability to be successful based on your own initiative. They reject the values and traditions that have made us great. They reject capitalism and the opportunity to become wealthy. They reject what America was, is, and can be again. I am not talking about democrats, I am talking about the left that has hijacked the Democratic Party.

In the end the idea that we need to tax the rich to fix the issues we face is simply a political tactic to divide and conquer, change our system of government, and reduce wealth and freedom. I have only touched the surface of this argument but if you have walked away from reading this book committed to analyze our political debates with more thinking and less emotion, I will have achieved my goal for this book.

There is no greater country to realize your dreams. I hope you realize that the ability to realize our dreams is put in jeopardy when we don't engage in the arguments. This country was founded by a small group of individual's committed to creating a government that protected the individual. It is your turn to protect the future of the greatest country ever devised by man.

Final footnote

The current politicians in congress both republican and democrat have sold this nation out. They have sold their votes to big business, big labor, big environment, big government, lawyers, billionaires, and have forgotten who they really work for. They work for us and you should never forget that. It is every American's responsibility to enforce the individual rights within our Constitution.

The first responsibility of every representative in congress is to swear an oath to protect the constitution. The failure of that duty deserves expulsion. Our founders would have physically and violently removed many of these politicians from office. They would have mixed feelings about how we as a people protected the system they gave us.

A few things they would be proud of:

- We ended slavery. The majority of founders knew that slavery was a stain on the America they envisioned.
- We used our economic power to spread freedom and opportunity around the world.
- The economic success so many people in the country and around the world derived from their simple concept of placing the power in the individual and not the government.
- They would be proud we are still a republic and have been stable since the civil war. They would have supported the civil war in concept but would have been divided on the method used to maintain the union.

A few things they would be disappointed by:

- The growth of the federal government overall.
- The staggering debt we have accumulated and the transfer of wealth forced through excessive taxation.
- The poverty and despair of the Black community. They would be surprised that such an industrious community would have been so dependent on government.
- The cronyism and self-centered actions of today's politicians. They would not be surprised that it was happening, they would be appalled at how the citizens were so accepting of it.
- They would be disappointed at the lack of patriotism and focus on diversity. They would love diversity but not at the cost of meritocracy and common sense.
- They would wonder how our Universities have fallen to such a level of political correctness at the expense of vibrant and vigorous debate.
- They would wonder how our immigration system went from bringing in people committed to the American Dream to people that had no intention of ever assimilating.
- They would not support a system that relied on "Taxing the Rich" and they would love this book!

I am only skimming the surface but I think they would give us a C+ overall. I think we can raise that grade by getting more involved with the process of government and elections. It is our individual duty to protect this the greatest nation ever devised by man. We should be proud of who we are from founding to today. We are a great people; each and every one of us!

ABOUT THE AUTHOR

Rich Hand is a dedicated husband and proud father of two grown children. He is a living advocate of the Founders of this nation and believes that the "American Dream" is in every individual's grasp no matter where they come from or what their circumstances are growing up. He loves writing songs, books, and notes to his family. He loves his dogs with all his heart and dreads the day his dogs will need his love to let them go. He knows his heart may not be able to take it. Until then he fills his heart with his best efforts to inspire people to live their life; Ignored!